I Choose You!

They Should Have NEVER Met

By Sam Troy

Copyright © 2023 Sam Troy

Print ISBN: 979-8-218-27287-6

All rights reserved. No portion of this document may be reproduced in any form without expressed, written consent from the author. I have tried to recreate events, locales and conversations from my memories of them. In order to maintain their anonymity in some instances I have changed the names of individuals and places, I may have changed some identifying characteristics and details such as physical properties, occupations and places of residence.

Dedication

This book is dedicated to my beauty, my darling son, Jack. May this book bring wisdom and understanding to all who read it.

Contents

Introduction vii
Jack's Life Begins 1
  Homeless With Jack 4
Aunt Liz's Shady Drama Began 15
Jack and I Finally Get A Break 24
Jack's First Day of School 29
Jack's First Car, College, and Apartment 33
The Jezebel Spirit Enters Jack's Life 37
The Jezebel Drama Begins 43
Next Level Disrespect 49
The Jezebel Resurfaces 55
Jack Moves With the Jezebel Spirit 59
Jack's Offer 63
New House Drama 66
The Beginning of the End 69
Jack's Peace Offering 84

Jack is Feeling Hopeless	87
Jack Accepts the Separation	90
The Final Days of Jack's Life	97
My Jack is Gone	107
Conclusion	111
Red Flags!	117
Final Thoughts	124

Introduction.

This book is written as a tribute to the life and memory of my son, who I will call Jack for the sake of his privacy. My beautifully created love passed away a few years ago, which broke my heart in ways you could not imagine! However, after taking some time to grow into how to deal with the new reality of him not being here with me any longer, I feel it is my obligation to share his story with hopes that it will help others who may be in a similar situation.

All of the information revealed in this book

is based on my actual conversations with Jack, and my observation of him as these events were taking place.

Before I unfold Jack's incredible story, I want to share a bit about our background together as mother and son so you can get an understanding of who he was and how much he means to me.

I Choose You!!

Chapter 1.

Jack's Life Begins

When I was 15 years old, I became pregnant with Jack. And I know you are probably wondering, "Why were you pregnant at 15?" Well, back in the 80s, there were people in the world who did not talk with their kids about sex, and unfortunately for me, my parents were a part of those people!

In our ignorance, my 17-year-old boyfriend Neal and I committed the act of sex for the first time. The next thing I knew, I was throwing up in my mother's car. Shortly after, I found out that I was pregnant.

I Choose You!!

I gave birth to Jack the same year that I turned 16. While recovering in the hospital room, Neal and I were waiting for the nurse to bring the baby in so we could hold him and see him. As I lay there waiting to see my baby, I started to wonder what he looked like and what it was going to be like being a mother. I also was thinking about the pain I had just gone through in having him.

A few hours after I had Jack, the nurse brought him in to meet us. As soon as I first laid eyes on him, I didn't even think about the pain any longer because I was captured by the sight of my new baby I had been waiting for so long to see!

A smile suddenly came over my face as I met my little one. He was fair-skinned, had straight black hair, a long, little body, and he was still wrinkled from being in my belly. I didn't care about his little wrinkles because he was what I called "My Beauty."

Several days after I gave birth to Jack, we were discharged from the hospital and went home to stay with my mother where four of my other siblings were living as well, including my eldest brother, Drew, who was two years older than me.

The initial months of baby Jack and I living with my mother were good, and Jack was what I called a good baby. Although I had to get up a couple of times during the night to feed and change him, he was not a whiny baby at all.

My mother was not happy about Neal and I getting pregnant and having a baby, but she embraced Jack and "seemed" to be happy we were living with her. She even allowed Neal to come to visit with us. My mother worked nights and pretty much slept all day, so we rarely saw her anyway.

However, as the months went on, my mother became more and more aggravated with us living in her house. Not just Jack and I but my brother Drew as well. Then, one day out of the blue, the explosion came!

Chapter 2

Homeless With Jack

After about seven months of Jack and I living with my mother, she one day without warning announced to me and Drew that she wanted us to get out of her house. When she made that first announcement, I thought to myself that she was on some kind of temporary trip. Surely, she was not expecting me to leave that house with a seven-month-old baby and nowhere to go!

So, in response to her outburst, I continued on with what I was doing. Well, that was until the second public announcement sounded off with a more aggressive pitch than the first one. She stood up and screamed, "Get out of my house NOW!"

Drew and I both knew she was serious, and the one thing we knew about our mother is that she was not one to mess around with. She was a tall, stout woman who was mean and absolute about everything she said. So, when she stood up repeating that she wanted us out of her house, we knew that she meant right then, not that night, the next day, or even the next week. She wanted us to go right at that very *second*!

{Side Bar: We had no clue why our mother was acting this way. Looking back years later, we just charged it to the fact that maybe there were too many people in her house, including kids, and she was tired of it all.}

Anyway, because we knew that my mother was not about to take any sassy backtalk from her kids, Drew and I didn't even attempt to push back on her demand for us to get out of her house. Instead, we just looked at each other in dismay and started packing up the few items we had. Within an hour, we left with baby Jack as we were told.

Together, with my seven-month-old baby, we left her house for the streets! At this time, I had just turned 17. I had no money; I didn't even have a stroller to carry Jack in. Luckily, my brother was there with me, so he and I took turns carrying Jack.

After about an hour or two of walking, carrying Jack back and forth, and trying to hold on to the few other items we had, my brother spotted a stray grocery buggy across the highway. He ran across the busy highway and grabbed the buggy so we could carry Jack and our belongings much easier.

We loaded Jack and the few clothing items into the buggy and continued off into the city streets. We were wandering around the streets aimlessly with nowhere to go, and I mean *nowhere* to go! Back then, neither my brother nor I had any knowledge of homeless shelters, and as far as we know, we were just fucked in the whole situation.

As we were walking, my brother and I were racking our brains trying to think of *anyone* we could call that would care enough to let us stay with them. This was becoming more and more concerning as darkness was closing in on us. We thought and talked and thought and talked, then suddenly, after wandering around the streets for so many hours, my brother came up with an idea of someone he thought was a good idea to call.

When my brother said he had someone in mind, my face lit up with excitement. "Who?" I asked. "Who are you thinking about?"

He hesitated, but he could tell I was eager to know who he was thinking about. A few seconds later, he softly said the name, "Aunt Liz."

He said the name so low that I had to repeat what I thought he said just to make sure I heard him right. When I repeated the name, and he said yes, all the happiness I felt rapidly dissipated from my face and body. A deep, curdling sickness in the pit of my stomach took its place.

She was the *last* person I would have thought of calling on this earth. For me, she was not even a thought and for sure nowhere *near* being a phone call for help!

I felt this way because our Great Aunt Liz was so mean and condescending, and I just *knew* she wouldn't let us stay with her—especially not *me* as a teenage mother. In my eyes, calling her was unbelievable! To me, this was not a great idea at all, and all I could think of is how much she hated me and would make my life a burning, living hell in her house.

I was not happy at all, but still, my brother insisted on calling her, saying it would be okay. He reassured me that he would make the call and told me not to worry! He was hopeful that she would have mercy and allow us to stay with her. Although I was desperate for shelter and care for my little Jack, the thought of calling Aunt Liz was nauseating, to say the least. Because, in all honesty, Aunt Liz was a total BITCH!!

When I say bitch, I mean you couldn't be around her without her making you feel like shit under the bottom of her shoe. She is that one relative in the family who, because she made a good life for herself, lived in a neighborhood with expensive homes, and had loads of money, would look down on other people in the family, but mostly the young people. In all the years I have known her, I've *never* observed her having a kind word to say to or about any young person, including me!

She made family gatherings a nightmare with her sharp tongue and condescending remarks. When she entered the room, most of the room would clear out because as soon as she saw someone she deemed as not put together, the breaking down of their self-esteem and confidence would begin. She would start cutting right into them with no hesitation.

For example, let's say someone in the family or maybe a friend of the family is happy with themselves and living their best life, but to her, they are overweight and on the chunky side. As soon as she saw that person, she would say something along the lines of, "You should be ashamed to be walking around with all that hanging off you."

She didn't care how the person felt about what she was saying or who was there to witness it. Basically, you would be a standing target for her while she threw verbal knives straight through you. She did all this while the other older relatives—her cheerleaders—would be standing by, watching and laughing at the show!

So, considering Aunt Liz's behavior and knowing her for other instances with anyone within her range, I was in no way, shape, or form rushing to call this lady for shelter! Also, it had not been long since my brother had come out of the closet announcing himself as being gay, and I was unsure if she was privy to this information.

I couldn't help but think, *This is not going to be good!* I could only imagine to myself how the witch, Aunt Liz, was going to have a field day gnawing on this one. She and her cheerleaders were going to have a good time grinding us up in their verbal grinder!

{Side Bar: This was the 80s, and during those days, being gay was still considered somewhat taboo. Although my brother was tough and confident in who he was, it was still a very sensitive subject from an acceptability standpoint. Given Aunt Liz's demeanor, I was concerned for the treatment of my brother if she found out this information while we were in her house!}

Nevertheless, my brother, Jack, I, and the grocery buggy headed to the phone booth for the dreaded call to Aunt Liz. The closer we got to the phone booth, the more anxious I became. My brother could see this and kept reassuring me that this *was* a good idea.

The phone booth was about two blocks away. Once we got there, I intensely watched my brother pick up the phone receiver with one hand while reaching into his pocket with the other, searching for money to make the call. He pulled a dime and two pennies out of his pocket, put the dime into the phone, and started dialing her number.

The dial tone seemed to take forever, and then I heard him say, "Hello, Auntie, this is Drew." He then started explaining our situation. The whole time he was on the phone, I was standing there—a bag of nerves. Part of me was thinking, *Please say yes,* and another part of me was thinking, *This witch is not going to say yes, she hates me!*

As I was standing there anxiously holding my breath, I suddenly looked down into the buggy, and there was Jack—staring up at me with a big smile on his face. I saw my beautiful baby boy so innocent and carefree. After seeing Jack's face, I wanted nothing more than for Aunt Liz to say YES. I just wanted to get my baby off the streets.

I couldn't hear what she was saying on the other end of the phone, but I could hear my brother explaining our situation. When he was silent, I knew she was talking. He was responding with a straight face, saying, "Okay, okay," "I know," "Yes ma'am," and "No ma'am." Hearing these responses from my brother made me concerned. What was she saying?

After about 20 minutes, the call ended, and he hung up. After Drew put the phone on the receiver, I stood there, trying to decipher his facial expression to see if he was happy or sad. I couldn't tell.

He slowly walked ahead of me with his head down. "She said no," he replied in a low voice. This time, I knew exactly what Drew had said, and I immediately dropped my head as well in disappointment. What were we going to do now, for real?

I Choose You!!

Then, my brother playfully ran ahead, laughing and saying aloud, "Sike! She said yes! She said yes!"

I joined him with the buggy and burst into my own laughter. We both took a deep breath and went off to Aunt Liz's house. My brother said Aunt Liz didn't hesitate to say yes to letting us stay with her. In fact, she was delighted with the idea of having a baby in the house!

Chapter 3.

Aunt Liz's Shady Drama Began

We arrived at Aunt Liz's house just before dark. My brother eagerly led the way up the stairs to her porch, but I was still feeling somewhat uneasy about the whole idea of living with her. My pace slowed down as we approached her door. My brother rang the doorbell, and about a minute or so later, the door swiftly opened. There she was, Aunt Liz, with a big grin on her face, holding the door open as we entered her house.

Initially, things were okay at Aunt Liz's. She welcomed us in but was especially joyful over baby Jack being there. You would have thought *she* had just had a baby with how overly excited she was with him. Although she was welcoming to me and Drew and treated Jack kindly, there were moments when she would still make little comments with the negative connotations she was famous for. However, knowing this is who she was, we would ignore those remarks for the time being for the sake of peace and having somewhere for us to live.

As the weeks went on, she started to reveal more and more of her true self, and then eventually, the real Aunt Liz showed up! She started with my brother Drew first, but this time, she wasn't as blatant as she normally was and called herself being slick about it.

Typically, when she was on the phone, she'd be in her bedroom with the door closed. Sometimes, we could hear her talking and laughing but not necessarily understand what she was saying. However, on "It's Time To Fuck With Drew" day, she intentionally left her bedroom door open so we could clearly overhear her conversation.

At first, we thought it was just her usual gossip about everybody else's business and paid it no mind. That was until her voice got louder, leaving us no choice but to hear what she was saying. As we listened more closely, it was clear that this conversation was *exclusively* about Drew.

Amongst other things, she was going on and on about how she had heard about Drew saying he was gay and that he should have kept his being gay business to himself. She mentioned how she wondered how our father and grandfather would feel when they got wind of this news.

Overhearing Aunt Liz talking about him, Drew got livid. He was not one to hold back how he felt, and I noticed him heading towards her bedroom, saying, "I'm about to let the bitch have it!" As bad as I wanted somebody to get this bitch told, I know that if Drew was the one who delivered this much-needed "Put Aunt Liz In Her Place" act, we would not only be put back on the street with Jack but also frowned upon by other family members for what they would deem as being disrespectful to Aunt Liz.

To avoid this from happening, I picked up baby Jack, gripped Drew's hand, and led him outside. We walked to the corner store, and on the way there, I pleaded with Drew not to argue with Aunt Liz so we wouldn't be back on the streets again.

It was not easy to calm Drew down, but he eventually relaxed and said that *because* Jack and I needed somewhere to live, he wouldn't say anything to Aunt Liz about over-hearing her talking about him on the phone. But because she had one more time to fuck with him, he was going to find somewhere else to go!

Over the next few weeks, Drew would stay out late or not come to Aunt Liz's at all some nights. One day, he just left and never came back. When Drew told me he was not coming back, I felt sick again. This time was much worse than when he first mentioned her name as the person to call for shelter. Now it was just me and Jack trapped in the rapture of Hurricane Liz. What is she going to do to me now that Drew is gone?

During the time all of this was going on, Aunt Liz was about 70 years old. Prior to letting us move in with her, she had a boyfriend named Melvin, who would visit her quite frequently. After we arrived, he did not visit as much. I'm not sure what his living situation was, but she never visited him when I was living there with her.

In any case, it was apparent that she was feeling some kind of way about her man not visiting like he used to. She also didn't have the privacy that she was used to, which evidently was a problem.

It was obvious that she'd had enough of not having the privacy she was so desperately seeking. I knew this because she had clearly reached her no-privacy breaking point the day she abruptly shouted, "No more damn privacy! I like sex too!" while slamming her bedroom door.

The bedroom where Jack and I slept and spent most of our time was adjacent to her bedroom. Therefore, I no doubt could hear the outburst, and unfortunately for me, it was at this point that I knew it was my turn! Instead of her being as cold and heartless as my mother was in putting us out of her house right then, Hurricane Liz's strategy for making my life a living hell was to dig inside her playbook of ratchetness. Her tactic was to run one of her favorite all-time plays, which by the way, was the same play she ran on Drew, but with an added dirty twist!

Negative and condescending she was as she began to complain about any and everything I did, I said, and how I was raising Jack. Whatever she could think of was what she would use as an opportunity to attack me, and when she couldn't think or witness anything, she just started making up lies.

At first, she tried the same BS that she did with Drew, which was leaving her bedroom door open while she was resting comfortably on her bed, talking negatively about me on the phone with her usher board church members who were a part of her cheerleader team as well.

Then, she escalated as she started to invite her supporters over for whiskey and gossip time. These are the same people who condoned her mean behavior and thought she was funny when she was rude to others. In their whiskey and gossip sessions, they all would gather at the kitchen table, sipping whiskey from her expensive Chinaware and talking about me as if I was not there.

Oh, they were having themselves a *good* ole time while audaciously gossiping about how I was "fast and hot-tailed," and this was why I was a teenage mother. They were even questioning each other and asking, "Where the baby daddy?"

Hearing all this going on right there in the kitchen made me furious. Just like Drew, I wanted nothing more than to let all of these gossiping bitches have it! I did not have a problem doing it, but because I had Jack and knew we needed somewhere to stay, I would just go into the bedroom with my baby and close the door.

What her supporters *didn't* know was that Jack's dad had joined the Army. Therefore, he could not be there; however, Aunt Liz *knew* this because she had to have the 411 the first day I entered her house. Nevertheless, she carried on as if she had no clue. I guess she kept quiet to make for a better gossiping session. She was just dirty, and all I wanted to do was get the hell out of her house!!!

She made sure I heard *everything* she said about me. It sounds horrible, but this was Aunt Liz being Aunt Liz. Remember, I mentioned earlier how she had a reckless mouth, and she said what she wanted without caring who was listening or how they felt about it. So, what did I expect, right? Exactly, I *knew* this was coming!

At this point, all I could think of was what I was going to do to get out of there and avoid being homeless with Jack again. My biggest worry each day was what I was going to do!

I knew that being homeless with my baby was not an option again. I had experienced that already when Drew was with me, but now that he was gone, it was just Jack and me. There was no way I could handle it on my own! The only other choice I had at that time was to continue to deal with the mental anguish Aunt Liz was serving me each day!

Chapter 4.

Jack and I Finally Get A Break

A month went by after Drew left Jack and me all alone with Aunt Liz. By now, I was pretty much used to her coming for me and just tried my best to stay out of her way.

Feeling hopeless about the whole situation, I decided to call my sister Kelly, who is one year older than me, to see how things were going with her. While talking with her about what was going on at Aunt Liz's house and how she ran Drew away, Kelly said she suspected that was going to happen given what we had already witnessed with Aunt Liz's reckless conduct.

Concerned about Aunt Liz's treatment of me and possibly Jack later down the line, Kelly mentioned how her child's father's sister had helped her to get into a program for government assistance and that she now had an apartment that was being paid for, was getting food stamps to buy food, and had something called WIC where you could go get free baby formula.

Now, reader, you can probably imagine how excited I was to hear this coming from the other end of the phone. I was excited and thought to myself that if *I* could only get this government assistance program, I would finally be able to get the H to the E to the double hockey sticks away from Aunt Liz!! Can I get a hallelujah and an AMEN!!!!! I would have a place to call home for me and my baby, and I'd no longer have to worry about us living on the street. Wherever this government assistance is, please sign me up!!

This was the best news I had heard in a long time, and after getting off the phone with Kelly, I felt relieved and hopeful that I would be leaving the whole living with Aunt Liz nightmare behind me! I started envisioning Jack and me in our new home to the point where I didn't even see or hear Aunt Liz any longer, even when she was right in front of me.

The next day, my sister and I went to the government agency, and I applied and was approved for the government assistance program. She also helped me find a small apartment, and before you knew it, Jack and I moved into our new home!

Oh, Aunt Liz *pretended* to be sad to see us leaving her house, but I knew *that* was a lie! Anyway, Jack and I were finally away from that madness. We were safe with just he and I together. We settled in quickly, and Jack was such a good baby. He was walking by this time and never gave me any problems, not even when I would sit his little baby bottom on the big toilet for potty training.

He was potty trained by 11 months, which I was grateful for because resources were limited. It helped not to have to worry about buying diapers for my little one again.

Jack and I lived in the apartment for a few years. With Kelly and Drew helping me to watch Jack, I could go to a business trade school a couple of days a week. At the trade school, I learned the skills of typing and medical billing. After eight months, I graduated top of the class and even received an honorary award for my achievement.

The trade school also helped me find a job in the medical billing field, which was a true blessing. Jack and I were doing good, so good that after a year or so of working, I was able to get off government assistance completely.

I saved up enough money to buy us a used

car to get around in, and we had it going on. At least, that's how I felt at that time.

Chapter 5.

Jack's First Day of School

A few years went by, and now it was time for me to put my little guy in school. For me, this was a tough one because while I was excited for Jack to be going to school, I was also sad at the same time. He and I had been together for four years, just him and me. Now, it was time to send my beauty into a new environment he didn't know with people he *also* did not know!

I was absolutely feeling some kind of way about taking my Jack into this unknown world, but although this was how I felt, Jack was ready! His first day of school outfit consisted of dress pants, a dress shirt, and some Stacy Adams look-alike shoes, which he later named "Hollywoods."

Walking Jack into the school on the first day was intense, but Jack was not scared at all. If he was, I surely could not tell by the way he pimped-walked into the school with all the confidence in the world. It was like he *knew* they were waiting for him and that he was the star of the class already.

When I saw how Jack was taking on his first day of preschool, it made me relax and let him be a big boy. Jack was a little man already showing his mom how little men handled the first day of school! Although I was so proud of Jack and happy to see him embracing his first day of school, I secretly cried in the car on my way home.

When I picked Jack up from his first day of school, the teacher said he did good in class and did not give her any problems. Jack said he had a good time and was excited about going back the next day. So, we celebrated his first day of school at Chuck E. Cheese.

After graduating from preschool, Jack excelled through elementary school. He even became his 5th-grade teacher's favorite student. During a PTA meeting, I questioned how Jack was doing with his schoolwork and in the class overall. His 5th-grade teacher said she took a liking to Jack not only because he excelled in his schoolwork but because she admired how he was always willing to help the other classmates.

Hearing this made me so proud of Jack, but I was not surprised because he always had a kind heart and willingness to help others. Even at his young age, he would not only assist his classmates and family members but would help neighbors with taking their groceries in the house, assist elderly neighbors in doing yard work, and perform other random acts of kindness.

He would do these things with a smile on his face and not expect anything in return.

Therefore, when his teacher mentioned this about Jack, I was not at all shocked. Once he got to high school, Jack became interested in modeling. At first, I didn't think he was as serious about it, but once he showed me that he had a *true* interest, I supported him. He and I would travel multiple times a year back and forth to other cities including Chicago, Illinois, for modeling auditions. He even appeared in a couple of local magazines.

Chapter 6.

Jack's First Car, College, and Apartment

As much as I wanted Jack to go to college straight after high school, he decided to try life out without college for a while. He worked at a well-known local food chain for a few hours a week when he was in high school, but his first job after graduating was at a local hardwood store. He enjoyed it so much that he would work extra hours because his dream was to save up enough money to buy a car.

In the first year of working at the hardware

and putting in extra hours, Jack was able to save up enough money to buy his first car. Although the car was used, it was new to Jack. It was his first car, he paid cash for it, and he was excited about his new ride!

On the day he first bought the car, I had no clue that he had it until he came home. He was so thrilled, calling out to me, "Mama, where you at? Come here, I got something to show you!!" I ran to the front of the house, and there Jack was with a big smile on his face. He grabbed my hand, and we ran outside together. When we got outside, I glanced over to the driveway and saw a shiny vehicle, freshly washed with the wheels all shined up. It was Jack's first car!

I was so happy and shared in the excitement with Jack. I remember at that moment reflecting back on when he was a baby, our homeless struggle, and here he was now—a grown man, working and just bought his first car. I was absolutely a proud mother!!

And you know the next thing we had to do, right? That's right, Take it for a spin!

***

After Jack brought his first car, he picked up a second job and a year later was able to get his own place. He moved into an apartment not too far from me. Jack was enjoying his car and his new place; he was even dating.

A couple of years into him having his own place, he expressed to me how he was finally thinking about going to college but that he could not afford to pay rent and attend college at the same time. Therefore, he wanted to come home until he completed his degree. Of course, I said yes.

So, in 2008, Jack came home to live with me and applied to one of the top universities in our state. When he was accepted, he made it clear that he had no plans on spending 10 years in college. I watched him diligently focus on his coursework. He did well and graduated with a four-year degree in four years flat! My child was determined. As you can probably imagine, I was extremely pleased with him and how he had grown up to be a beautifully spirited, responsible man.

After graduating college, Jack applied for several professional jobs, including one position in particular that he was interested in, which was with our local government. While in the process of applying for and landing his dream job, Jack found another job that paid him well enough that he was able to move out on his own again, getting another small apartment.

Jack was doing so good for himself, prospering like any other young man through life. Everything was going so well for him until that Jezebel spirit manipulated her way into my baby's life!

Chapter 7.

The Jezebel Spirit Enters Jack's Life

As I mentioned earlier, Jack was dating occasionally, but it had not been anything too serious. I suspect this is because he was primarily focused on his career and work. One day I remember Jack calling me, saying, "Ma, I'm stopping over after work. What did you cook?"

"I haven't started cooking yet," I explained, "but I plan on making one of your favorites—chicken and waffles." He was chuckling with excitement to hear I was making one of his favorites. When he was growing up, I often made breakfast-type meals for dinner, so this wasn't anything out of the norm.

Jack arrived at my house around 6:45 p.m. I heard the door open while I was still cooking in the kitchen.

"Hey, Ma," he greeted me as he kissed me on the cheek before heading to the bathroom. When he returned, we sat down in the dining room to eat, and I noticed he had the biggest grin on his face.

"What are you grinning about?" I asked.

At first, he was a bit hesitant to say, so I asked again. "What are you smiling about?"

He then said, "Well, I met this girl on the Internet a couple of months ago, who I really like. The only thing is, I'm not sure if she feels the same about me." Jack explained that he was unsure if she felt the same because he had asked this girl about being exclusive, and she replied that she was talking with several men on social media and had not decided on who she was going to be exclusive with yet! Essentially, she was in the process of seeing which one she was going to choose. So, he was waiting to hear back from her on whether *she* was going to choose *him*.

When I heard Jack say he was waiting on *her* to choose *him*, the words "Choose *you*?" flew right out of my mouth before I could even think twice about how to respond to what I thought was nonsense.

Hearing this prompted a series of questions for me. "Who is this person, and why are you waiting on someone to choose *you*?" As his mother, I thought these questions were warranted because I knew my child and how I raised him to love and respect himself first, outside of God, of course!

He told me her name, but I will call her Amber for her privacy. Jack reiterated that he had met her on social media, was interested in her, and was waiting for her decision on whether she would choose him!

When Jack repeated what I thought I heard the first time, I replied, "She must be something really special to have several men on hold for her decision on who is the "chosen one."

I also wondered why Jack—who is not only university-educated but also cover-book handsome—would allow himself to be put in such a situation. I couldn't comprehend why he was waiting in a lineup to be chosen by some random girl on social media.

For the sake of me, I could not understand this, but Jack did not seem to have a problem with it. So, I resorted to the mindset of thinking I was just old-fashioned. *Oh, okay,* I thought. *Maybe this is how young people meet these days, and this is the process of online dating, waiting to be chosen!!*

A couple of weeks passed before Jack said Amber had decided who she would be exclusive with and revealed that he *was* the chosen one. Upon hearing this from Jack, curiosity got the best of me, and I asked him, "How exactly did she say it?"

He said he received a message from her via Facebook with the words: "I CHOOSE YOU!"

Of course, when I heard the "I CHOOSE YOU" play, I thought to myself how this was such poppycock! The whole situation seemed suspicious to me, and I was feeling some way about this entire thing. What *were* those feelings? I didn't know at the time, but I knew it was something!

Nevertheless, Jack seemed thrilled about Amber's decision to choose him. So, I accepted it and put my suspicions aside… for now!

{Side Bar: Thinking back on the "I Choose You," I do not believe there was a flock of men on Facebook waiting for Amber to choose them. It is my belief that this was a play that she ran in order

I Choose You!!

to get men to think she was highly sought after, making herself more desirable!}

Chapter 8.

The Jezebel Drama begins

A week or so after Amber revealed to Jack that he was the chosen one, she invited him over to the "family house" to meet her in person along with other family members, including her 5-year-old daughter. Shortly after the visit, he gave me a call. When I answered the phone and heard his voice, I could tell something was wrong. So, I asked him, "How did the visit go?"

"I guess it was okay," he said softly. He elaborated by saying how the visit was not what he was expecting and that he was somewhat disappointed in how Amber greeted him and her behavior toward him in front of her family.

Jack went on to explain that when he got to Amber's house, he did not see anyone that looked like her outside with the other people. So, he texted her to let her know he was there.

She texted back that she was on her way out, but after 20 minutes or so of waiting, she *still* had not come out to greet him. The whole thing felt like it was intentional; he could hear her and her other family members talking and laughing inside the house.

Jack continued to say that when Amber *did* come out of the house, she started making sarcastic remarks towards him, bossing him around, and being condescending. He said it came across as her trying to show off in front of her family, treating him as if he was weak or some kind of sucker she could dog around.

When Jack told me about what happened at this girl's house, to be honest, I was not one bit surprised, especially given the way she went about getting him in the first place with the whole "I CHOOSE YOU" scheme.

I told Jack this was not a nice way to treat someone after inviting them to your home! I also told him that he should think seriously about getting more involved with this girl because if she showed that behavior on the *first* visit, what's next?

I said to Jack that people can be one person on social media and a whole other person when you actually *meet* them. Jack said he would talk with Amber to see where that behavior towards him came from and if this was something he had to be concerned about going forward. I told him to tread lightly with this one because she was a total suspect for a HAM (Hot Ass Mess!)

Jack said that he had overlooked the fact that Amber lived in one of the most destitute areas in the city and that the neighborhood and the house she and her family lived in were run down. He also observed that the front door on the house was broken and being held closed with some kind of rope. It was apparent that Amber and her family had financial issues.

Over the next week or so, Jack said he and Amber had a talk about the visit, and she expressed that she was just playing around with him and apologized for her behavior. Jack said he had accepted her apology because he had not seen this side of her before and figured maybe she *was* just joking around, so the relationship went on.

After a few weeks of dating, Jack learned that Amber was not working and was in school to become a nurse assistant. Of the six or seven adults living in the "family house," only two of them had jobs. It was even more obvious that they were in a financial strain.

Jack had a kind heart, and although he was not financially wealthy, he wanted to help in any way he could. So, he went to the hardwood store, bought the materials needed to fix the broken front door lock, and fixed it himself.

After he fixed the broken lock on the door, Jack said that Amber and her family seemed to be grateful. However, he later realized that fixing the door lock may not have been the best idea because Amber's family apparently started thinking that since Jack really liked her, he would do *anything* to please her!

This thought was proven by the way Amber's mother (Patty) and her boyfriend—who Jack later learned both loved to smoke cigarettes and drink liquor daily—started asking him for things like rides to the store, and money to buy liquor and cigarettes. They would even ask *him* for cigarettes, although they never saw him smoking. They *knew* he didn't smoke, but they also knew he liked Amber and used this as a token to get stuff from him.

The mother and boyfriend were not the

only ones starting to take advantage of him. Amber started revealing that disrespectful behavior again as well. However, this time it was *next-level* disrespect!

Chapter 9.

Next Level disrespect

Amber's 25th birthday was coming up the following month, so she started planning to have a party. As expected, she asked Jack to help fund it. She picked out the location, asked his advice on the decorations, and acted like she valued his input.

Being the sweet man he was, he gave her everything that she asked for, including money to buy her birthday party outfit. He even paid Patty to watch Amber's child on the day of the big event. A few days prior to the birthday party, Jack had also gone out and bought Amber a gift for her birthday that he planned to give to her at the party. As far as he knew, everything was good.

Unfortunately for Jack, all was *not* good because Amber had other intentions for her party when it came to him. She turned what should have been a drama-free event into one *full* of drama and disrespect.

A couple of days before the party, Amber revealed to Jack that she did not want him to come. When Jack asked why, she told him she was going to have some friends there, including her ex-boyfriend. Since this ex-boyfriend might be "entertaining" her, she did not want him to be jealous.

Now, reader, if you are anything like me, I know you are probably thinking, *What in the you have lost your damn mind is going on here?*

Anyway, Jack asked Amber, "What are you going to be doing at the party that I, as your man, will be jealous of?" Amber reiterated that she and her ex-boyfriend were still good friends, and he was going to be at the party.

Jack then asked Amber if the ex-boyfriend was her child's father because, if so, the reason for the invite to the party would make more sense. However, if that *wasn't* the case, why would she choose to have an *ex*-boyfriend come to the party and not the man she is *currently* dating?

When Jack asked, she told him that was not the case. The child's father had not been in the child's life for several years. So now, Jack saw the invitation to the ex as suspect, and he was feeling some kind of way about it—especially after he helped pay for the party, paid for the mother to watch her child, and paid for Amber's birthday gift.

Jack was upset, to say the least! But how he felt didn't matter to Amber; she was adamant about him not coming to her party. Seeing how Amber was treating him about the situation, Jack finally told her, "Fine, I won't come to the party!"

Jack was not happy at all about how Amber played him on the party invite. So, on the day of the party, Jack was trying to keep himself busy and not think about the party and what was probably going to be going on there between Amber and the so-called "ex-boyfriend." To keep himself busy and not concentrate on Amber and her birthday party mess, he picked up a few extra hours at work that would run into the time the party started. He knew he would be obligated to stay and finish the extra hours.

However, the closer it got to the time of the party, the closer Jack got to making a decision to show up at the party anyway after it had started to see exactly what was such a big deal with him being there. Jack said he knew he had the present already, so if he got to the party and Amber asked him why he was there, he would tell her that he wanted to give her the present *at* her party.

After deciding that showing up to the party *was* a good idea, Jack excitedly got dressed in the outfit he had already bought for the event before Amber gut-punched him with the whole uninvited crap. He grabbed the present and headed to the party. Along the way, Jack stopped and bought a bouquet of flowers to go with the present.

When he arrived at the party a couple of hours after it started, he could hear the music from outside. It sounded like everyone was having a good time. Jack walked into the party and started visually searching the room to see if he could locate Amber. After about a minute or so he spotted her. There she was—scantily clad sitting on some guy's lap. Jack figured the guy was the "ex-boyfriend," and *this* was why Amber didn't want him to come to the party. She wanted to be loose and disrespectful as hell behind his back!!

Upon approaching Amber, he could see she was having a good time on this guy's lap, laughing it up with a drink in her hand and a money necklace draping from her neck.

When she spotted Jack walking toward her, she didn't even bother to jump up from the guy's lap. When he reached her, she just looked at Jack and asked what he was doing there.

Jack stood there, rendered speechless for a moment. Although he was upset about what he was witnessing and how Amber blatantly disrespected him in front of everyone at the party who *knew* they were supposed to be a couple, he didn't show it. Instead, he left the party and Amber alone that night. He even blocked her number from his phone and blocked her on his social media accounts.

Chapter 10.

The Jezebel Resurfaces

When Jack finally got around to telling me about the whole birthday party situation, I had the same reaction I had when he told me about the visit to the family house to meet her in person for the first time. I was not surprised! I didn't say this to Jack, but I was happy to hear he had left that girl alone. I didn't have a good feeling about him getting involved with her after the whole "I choose you," crap.

***

I Choose You!!

A year or so had passed since Jack last saw Amber; he had changed jobs and moved into a different apartment. He had also started taking up some boxing classes, which was his favorite sport. All was good, Jack was good, and I was happy my son was out of that demeaning relationship. Life was moving on.

Until, Until, Until... One day, I asked Jack how his dating life was going and if he was seeing anyone. He said he was dating, but nothing serious. He also said he had run into Amber at a store, and she apologized for how she acted on her birthday. She made up a lame excuse that she had a lot going on, but she didn't give a solid explanation of why she treated him that way.

Jack said she gave him her phone number and asked him if he would give her a call because she wanted to talk to him about something.

She strategically avoided sharing *what* she wanted to talk about with Jack and just asked him to call her. Jack was so busy with work, his boxing classes, and the other things he had going on in his life that he forgot about Amber. Several months later, he ran into her again. She asked why he had not called, and Jack explained to her that he had been busy but would no doubt be giving her a call.

Due to our work schedules, Jack and I didn't get a chance to see each other that often, but we did make it a point to speak over the phone at least once or twice a week. About a couple of months after he said he had run into Amber, he and I were talking over the phone, and during the conversation, he said that he had something to tell me but didn't want me to be upset.

"I'm not going to be upset, what is it?" I asked. There was a moment of silence on the end of the phone. Then, Jack said that he had finally called Amber and they had had several conversations over the past few weeks concerning her behavior, including the first visit to the house, the party, and other things that were going on in their relationship.

Jack said Amber had convinced him that she would change and with this, he decided to give the relationship another chance.

What I was hearing from Jack was concerning, and an eerie feeling came over me. I couldn't put my finger on what it was exactly, but based on this girl's past behavior, I was worried! Still, I tried my best to allow Jack to live his life.

Chapter 11.

Jack Moves With The Jezebel Spirit

Now that Jack and Amber are back together to give the relationship another try, they both decided to not only delete their Facebook accounts but also agreed not to be on any social media platforms *at all*.

The relationship was not perfect. They still had some minor spats here and there, but they agreed to stay together and work through them. Also, the mama and her man resumed their begging shenanigans again,

I Choose You!!

asking Jack for money, rides to the store, etc.

After being back together for almost six months, Amber started complaining to Jack that she was tired of living in her crowded family house and wanted her own place. When Jack mentioned to me that they were discussing moving in together, I was thinking about how strange the idea was, particularly because as far as I knew, Amber was unemployed.

So first, I asked Jack what made them want to move in together. He explained how Amber said there were too many people staying in the family house and how she was grown with a child and wanted her own place. Unfortunately, she could not afford a place for herself and her child alone. She wasn't working, but she was planning to finish nursing assistance training.

Then, I asked the most question. "If she isn't working, who's going to be paying all the bills?"

Jack said, "For now, I'll cover the rent and some utilities, and Amber will use her government assistance to help with some utilities and food."

It was apparent that they had pretty much mapped out a plan for the financials and decided to move in together because she wanted to. Weeks after this conversation with Jack, I found out that he and Amber had in fact moved into a two-bedroom apartment together. He was working two jobs in order to keep up with the bills while she was allegedly finishing nursing assistance school.

After a year or so of living together, one of Jack's jobs cut back, and he was let go. Thankfully, he was still able to keep up with bills with the one job using the savings he had built up when he was just financially responsible for himself.

Within a couple of years of Jack paying the bills with one job and his savings, the savings account was depleted, and Amber was still not working. The rent was behind, the utilities were past due, and they were facing shut-off notices from the utility company along with an eviction notice from the apartment manager.

Seeing the notices made Jack somewhat distraught because he knew if something did not change soon, he and Amber would have to split up. By now he was used to living with Amber and her daughter as a family for several years, and he didn't want the family to have to live in separate places.

Chapter 12.

Jack's Offer

The possibility of splitting up what Jack deemed at this point as his family was concerning for him. Nevertheless, the date of eviction was coming up in the next few weeks, and it was time to go. On the day of the move, they were in the apartment packing up to go their separate ways when Jack decided to check the mailbox one last time before leaving the apartment completely.

Jack went down to the mailbox which was located in the lobby of the apartment building. He opened the mailbox, and in there was a big manila envelope smothering all the other mail. *What is this?* Jack wondered.

Eager to know what was in the big envelope, Jack opened it and read the first couple paragraphs of the letter that was inside. To his surprise, there was a job offer from the local government; it was the same one he had been waiting to hear from several years back when he first graduated from college. After applying and interviewing for the job, they had taken so long to respond that Jack had forgotten all about it.

Nevertheless, this put a big smile on Jack's face. He started to do a happy dance because he knew that his and Amber's financial troubles were over. He would be able to take care of them all with only one job and build up his savings again as well. He was so excited about what was revealed in the manila envelope and couldn't wait to share the news with Amber.

So, Jack rushed back into the apartment where Amber was still packing up for the move. He called out to her to see which room she was in and excitedly showed her the job offer. He was still smiling and happy about the job offer and the future to come; however, to his shock, Amber didn't seem to be happy about his good news at all! In fact, she downplayed it as if it was no big deal, stealing all of the bliss out of Jack's moment to share his good news with her.

He couldn't understand why Amber reacted this way. As a couple, she and her daughter would also benefit from the offer. However, when he told me about her response, I couldn't help but think that this response was nothing outside of envy and jealousy.

{Side Bar: Jack told me that this was not the first time Amber showed jealousy toward him. Normally, it would be when he would get dressed up to go out, even if it was with her! Why she was responding this way was baffling to me. Jack was a college graduate! Surely, she had to know his opportunity was going to come one day!}

Chapter 13.

New House Drama

Nevertheless, Jack carried on and started his new government job, which allowed them to move to another place together. This time, however, they were able to move into a two-bedroom house located near Amber's family's house.

I asked Jack why they didn't move to a nicer neighborhood, given he had a new job and could afford it. He said Amber did not want to move too far from her family. Big mistake!

After they moved into the new house, Amber got her nursing assistance certificate and started working at a local nursing facility with a 40-hour schedule. Not long after she started working at the nursing facility, she went to Jack and started to complain again, this time about working full-time.

Jack asked why she didn't want to work full time, and she expressed that the benefits she was receiving from government assistance, including medical benefits for her child, would be cut off if she kept working a 40-hour week.

To please Amber, he went along with what she wanted to do and allowed her to work part-time to keep her government benefits. With Amber working part-time hours, her contribution to the household was to pay one utility bill and help buy food; these were the only financial responsibilities she had in the house.

Amber was working part-time 2–3 days a week at a nursing facility on the afternoon shift, and Jack's new job required him to work a slightly earlier afternoon shift as well.

Jack and Amber were in the new house, and things seemed to be going well outside of small arguments/disagreements here and there. They also had a financial system that worked for them.

Chapter 14.

The Beginning of the End

After two years of living together in the new house, Jack and Amber had settled in and seemed to be doing okay. They had occasional quarrels, but again they were working through them together.

Then one day, while they were having a conversation, Amber mentioned that her favorite sister, Teri, who lived with her husband and their son, was planning on leaving her husband and moving back into the family house with the child.

At the time of having this conversation with Amber, Jack didn't think much of what Amber had said about her sister moving back. As far as he knew, it was just conversation. However, Jack's thoughts changed once Teri finally left her husband and moved back to the family house.

When Teri first moved back, Jack said he noticed shortly after that Amber would be gone away from home, spending more time than normal at the family house with Teri. He didn't make too much of it at first; but then as the weeks went on, he started observing that Amber's visits would be longer and longer.

He also could tell how those minor squabbles they'd sometimes encounter and work through together were now being exacerbated by Amber into more amped up arguments.

She would do this by blowing the most trivial situations out of proportion to create an excuse for her to leave for the family house.

She got so good at amping up the arguments that instead of being gone *hours* at a time at the house, she'd be gone for *days* at a time, making Jack feel as if he had treated her badly.

Jack knew Amber and Teri were close and liked spending time "kee-keeing" with each other, which he had no problem with; however, his issue was with how Amber would go about it with the whole turning what was clearly a minor argument into a full-blown major situation.

All this drama was caused so that she could storm off to the family house for a few days to hang out with Teri. Amber's leaving got so bad that most times, she was only willing to return home when Jack would go over to the family house and not only apologize to her in front of her family at her demand but borderline *beg* her to come home.

According to her, Jack was always the one wrong in these situations, not her! This is what she wanted to portray to her family, so she demanded for him to apologize in front of them. In their ignorance, they'd believed *he* was the villain. Jack was not one to argue, so for the sake of peace and for her to come home, he would oblige and apologize.

{Side Bar: In my opinion, this demanding Jack to apologize in front of her family resembled her behavior towards him on his first visit to meet her in person. This is also totally disrespectful to Jack, who took her and her child and put them in a house where she barely paid any bills. Also, allow me to give you a little more insight into Amber's previous living situation before moving in with Jack. Amber's family house had 5-6 bedrooms in which the mother and the four other sisters lived, including Teri. Apart from the mother, all these women were no older than 30 and unmarried. The one who was married (Teri) left her husband, and now he too had to visit her and their child at the house as well.}

Amber went to the house so often that it seemed like it was done purposefully. Jack couldn't quite figure it out, but it appeared that because Teri had left her husband and moved back to the house where there was no structure, no boundaries, and all the women in the house could do whatever they wanted whenever they wanted, Amber wanted to do the same. As a result, the dynamics of his and Amber's relationship shifted drastically!

Amber had resorted back to her earlier days of being next-level disrespectful. He one day ran across some provocative pictures of her on social media, which was egregious to him because, as far as he knew, he and Amber had agreed to delete their Facebook pages and not be on any social media platforms after they got back together.

So, why would Amber have the page in the first place? Secondly, why is she posting these trashy pics? He didn't understand! When he asked her about the picture and the Facebook page, it led to an argument and her leaving for the "house" once again.

Amber had manipulated the relationship dynamics to the extent that Jack no longer wanted to say anything to her about her behavior or anything she did for that matter. Because if he did, it would only create the perfect avenue for her to get upset, and he *knew* what came after that. Even if she did not leave, it was always a dangling threat.

Knowing she had this threat leverage in her back pocket, Amber would try every way possible to create drama in the relationship. For example, she had to be at work an hour earlier than Jack, which meant she would get ready and leave before him.

On the days she was scheduled to work, after getting dressed and ready to leave, she would be sure to go say bye to Jack, wearing attire that did not match what a nursing assistant would be wearing to work.

For example, she'd have on a low-cut blouse with a push-up bra and a piece of jewelry dangling between her breasts. She would also have on bright red lipstick, tight pants or a short skirt, and a blonde wig. Obviously, when Jack would see what she was wearing "to work," he would say something like, "I thought you were going to work." Of course, she would go into one of her tantrums, leave for work anyway, and not return after. These are the types of things she would do to upset Jack intentionally.

***

One day, Jack told me that he found something that made him sick, but he didn't want to say anything to Amber about it because he didn't want to start an argument.

"What is it?" I asked. "What has you so upset?" Jack then reached into his pocket and pulled out a notice of Amber's results from a clinic where she went to get tested for an STD that he knew nothing about! Although the STD results were negative, it was obvious Amber was cheating on Jack because if not, why would she be getting tested for an STD and not mention it to him so he could get tested as well?

Also, since Amber was manipulating some power over her and Jack's relationship with the whole "leaving for the house" threat, she introduced another calculating tactic into the drama of her antics. Now, Teri had taken on the role of her spokeswoman and decision-maker with anything regarding her and Jack's relationship. With the new role of Teri as Amber's relationship consultant, the communication between Jack and Amber was reduced to Teri being Amber's narrator.

The communication set up was that Amber would go to Teri with the problem, they would come up with a solution, and then Teri would relay to Jack what Amber was planning to do about the problem. She would tell him *if* Amber was coming home, *when* she was coming home, or if she was *not* returning home.

As you can imagine, Amber allowing Teri to be the catalyst in their relationship was hard for Jack to deal with and witness, especially with Teri being approximately five years younger than Amber. Amber was acting like *she* was the younger sister, and Teri, being a big part of their relationship, had become a bigger challenge for Jack to face.

To add to this, Jack noticed that when he would go to the house to visit with Amber, Teri's husband would be there as well, begging her to come home. Basically, she was using the family house as leverage to gain control over him as well.

It seemed this was the game these sisters were playing when they wanted to gain control over their relationship. There were no male or positive female mentors or role models for these women to learn how to treat the men they call themselves in a relationship with. They didn't understand that this behavior was not a good way to handle things when having issues in their relationships.

Jack was really frustrated with how the relationship was turning out, especially given

I Choose You!!

all the time, energy, and money he had put into trying to keep the relationship together. He was willing to do whatever Amber wanted him to do for her to return home and for their relationship to get better. So, although he didn't think he needed it, he agreed to take an anger management class at Amber's request.

{Side Bar: This is some real B.S. They have gained up on Jack using this house as leverage and now has him signing up for anger management, you have to be kidding me.}

Anyway, Jack was doing everything in his power to bring what he deemed as his family back together again, but it was clear that Amber was trying to manipulate Jack into believing he was the problem and not her. Truthfully, *she* was allowing outsiders to inject themselves into the relationship and causing more problems than normal.

It was obvious that Jack cared about the relationship and whatever Amber wanted, he would do his best to oblige. After he took her back, she said she wanted to move away from her family, so Jack moved into an apartment with her and her child and paid the bills. When she said she wanted a treadmill so she could start working on herself, he bought it. When she said wanted a $400 iWatch, he bought it. He even bought an engagement ring when she started badgering him about marrying her. He just hadn't given it to her yet!

{Side Bar: Keep in mind that prior to the sister returning home, Jack and Amber had been together for approximately six years. Did they have problems in the relationship? Yes, but without the outside forces, they were able to work through them together.}

***

Six months after Teri moved back to the house and the drama with Amber began, things were still the same. Amber would come home and run off when she was ready. Nevertheless, Jack was trying his best to be optimistic and keep a positive mindset about the relationship.

They would still go on outings together, but now Teri would make sure she and her husband tagged along. However, when it came time for the couple to pay for *their* part of the food and gas expenses, they never had any money, resulting in Jack paying for all the food and gas expenses just to keep the peace with Amber.

On one occasion, when they were traveling via Jack's car to a water park, they stopped to get gas. Amber and Teri's husband went into the store to get snacks, Jack got out of the car to pump the gas and then got back inside the car. Teri who was sitting in the back seat leaned forward to Jack and said, "Where did Amber find you? Where are all the other good men hiding?" As she was touching his shoulder, Jack said he had a "what the fuck" look in his eyes, hidden by his dark sunglasses. He just chuckled a bit while thinking, *WOW!*

The flirting didn't stop there! When they reached the water park and changed into their swim clothes, he caught her staring at him several times, even with her husband right beside her. After the trip to the water park, Jack felt uncomfortable around Teri.

He often caught her staring at him from across the room. When he would catch her eyes peering at him, she would suddenly look away. Anytime he and Teri would be alone in a room, she would make remarks such as "Cute smile," "Oh, you have pretty hair," and "I bet you'll make pretty babies."

Jack said he became more and more uncomfortable around Teri but was unwilling to say anything to Amber about Teri's questions, remarks, or stares because he knew she would accuse him of flirting with her sister, leading to *more* problems.

***

A couple of more months had passed when Jack and Amber got into another one of those minor arguments where Amber exacerbated the situation like she normally did and ran off to the house with Teri. It's funny because she had not fully moved back home anyway, always one foot in one foot out!

The first week that she was gone, Jack came to my house and told me everything that had been going on with Amber. He said he was tired of running after her for those past eight months since Teri had come back and was going to let her come home on her own this time.

After a week went by, Amber still had not returned home, so Jack tried to reach her by phone and email. She was not responding to either, and she had blocked his number. All this was confusing to Jack because they still had the house together and all her things were still there. Had she decided not to come back home? Did she not want her things? Jack didn't know!

A few more weeks went by, and Amber had not returned home and was still not answering Jack's calls, emails, or texts. As a last effort, Jack decided to go to the house to talk with Amber about the house they shared together and their relationship.

When he pulled up to the house, the mother and her man were sitting outside on the porch. As soon as they saw Jack getting out of the car, they started begging and quibbling with him that if he bought them X, Y, and Z, they would get Amber to come outside for him.

Chapter 15.

Jack's Peace Offering

Although she was refusing to return home, Amber would come out to speak with Jack during the first couple of trips he made to the house. It was apparent that Teri was encouraging Amber to leave Jack and come stay with her at the house so they could go out, have fun, and do whatever they wanted. Still, Jack was fighting for the relationship. As a last-ditch effort, he thought about how prior to leaving this last time, Amber had been asking for him to buy her a new car.

Jack said he didn't buy Amber a car because

she had one that worked *and* he was saving his money to buy them a house. That way, they would never have to worry about somewhere to live or getting evicted again. However, because he saw how stubborn Amber was about coming home, Jack decided this would be a good time to buy her the car she wanted. He figured that with this peace offering, she could buy the car and hopefully decide to come back home.

The next day, Jack went to his bank, withdrew the $15,000, and then headed to Amber's family house. He was optimistic along the way about things returning to normal with him and Amber. He turned the corner and could see the whole family mingling out front, which made him a bit uneasy. Still, he approached the house anyway. Amber was out on the porch as well, so he walked up to her and asked if he could speak with her privately.

"Whatever you have to say to me, you can say in front of my family," she said loudly. She always wanted her family to witness how much control she had in the relationship with Jack.

So, right there in front of the whole family, Jack confessed his love for Amber and presented the $15,000 peace offering to buy the car. At first, Amber seemed excited until she realized it was not enough to buy the car she wanted. So, she did not accept the peace offering. On top of that, she still refused to return to the home they had together.

As you can imagine, the family is there to witness Jack with the $15,000 peace offering and another one of Amber's rejections towards him. He could hear the family saying, "Damn, Amber! That man must really love you to give you that kind of money!"

Jack said he witnessed Amber with both of her index fingers pointed at her private area, saying, "It's this BAD-ASS PUSSY!"

Chapter 16.

Jack is Feeling Hopeless

Jack finally realized that Amber was not willing to cooperate with him no matter what he did. He was feeling foolish and embarrassed in front of her family once again, so he came home to stay with me for a while to get away from the whole messy situation.

Although Jack had been telling me bits and pieces of what was going on while they were unfolding, he was able to sit and explain the whole situation of how he and Amber's relationship started going downhill right after Teri returned to the family house. He explained how not only was Amber allowing her sister to inject herself into their relationship, but she also was controlling Amber's decisions.

After Jack revealed all the details, I advised him to allow Amber to do whatever she wanted to do. If she wanted to return home and be with him, she would! He needed to give her some time to think about what she was going to do. I told him that he showed her too much of how he felt about her, and that is why she was treating him this way. This was the way she knew how to treat men.

Also, I said that if he really wanted to know how Amber felt about him, just leave her alone. If the love was there, it would show up. I also warned Jack to beware that once he stopped chasing after Amber like he had been in the past each time she ran off to the house, she would try various ways to get his attention because she was not used to him NOT chasing after her!

So, Jack, who had always listened to the advice I gave him, stopped chasing after Amber. While it was a hard decision for Jack, he decided to surrender to the battle of trying to get Amber to come home.

Chapter 17.

Jack Accepts the Separation

A couple more weeks went by, and Jack still had not contacted Amber or chased after her. He was settling into his new routine of being by himself. He went to work each day and drove back and forth from my house to the house he and Amber shared so he could keep an eye on the place. All their things were still there, and he didn't want the neighbors to think no one was there at the house. Sometimes, he would sleep there just because.

At times, I could tell Jack was still bothered by the situation; but he was dealing with it as men often do, in silence. He was making a good effort to adapt to the new situation. I could tell because he even barbecued for the holiday and invited some family and friends over to the house. Naturally, Amber was not there!

Jack was adapting nicely to his new situation. Until, Until, Until… One day, he heard the sound of a text message notification on his phone. When he looked at it, he saw it was from Amber, sending him a list of items she would be moving from the house.

When Jack told me about the message, I said, "Just as I told you, as soon as you stop chasing after her, she would be doing whatever she could to get your attention, and this is exactly what this text message is all about. Getting your attention."

Seeing this message from Amber, Jack was somewhat disappointed because he did not want Amber to move; he just wanted her to realize how she was destroying their relationship. I told him not to worry about the message too much because I believed that it was just one of Amber's conniving ways to get him to come running over to that house to beg her not to move so she could reject him again. I advised Jack to just ignore the message so long as she did not list any of his things as being moved from the house.

Although it was a hard decision for Jack, he did not respond to the message from Amber. He went on with his life, working, going to the gym, attending boxing classes, and spending time with me on his off days.

Over the next couple of weeks, Amber would send multiple text messages to Jack, adding to the list of items she was taking from the house; however, because Jack had not responded, the threats of removing her things grew to having the cable and lights shut off.

Jack was perplexed about Amber's threat of having the cable and lights shut off, considering the fact that the bills were current. It had been a few weeks since the first message she sent stating that she was moving things from the house, but Jack, who was still going back and forth to check on the house, saw that she had not moved anything thus far.

So, Jack ignored the messages. Besides, the items she listed all belonged to her, so she was free to take them and have the cable and lights shut off too. Jack was okay with whatever Amber wanted to do as long as she did not try to remove any of his things from the house.

Jack continued with his life, trying not to think about the situation with Amber and the whole house madness. Still, she never stopped! She had been with Jack long enough to know his daily routine, including what time he left the house for work and where he usually stopped off to get snacks and gas if needed.

On one particular morning, after staying

overnight at their house, Jack headed to work. On his way, he stopped off around his typical time to get gas and snacks. While putting gas in the car, he just so happened to glance over across the street at the other gas station, and there was Amber, wearing practically nothing in her booty shorts and tank top, smiling, and talking with a guy.

Of course, seeing this bothered Jack, but he just observed it and went on to work anyway. It had been about two months since Amber left, and Jack was realizing the situation between them was not getting any better. Therefore, with everything going on with her, including her acting like she was no longer capable of handling her issues with him directly, the rejection, and the disrespect, Jack grew tired of it all and decided it was time for *him* to move on and leave the house they'd once called home too.

Jack started looking for an apartment, which took about a month before he found one he liked. After securing the apartment, he got his move-in date and then started shopping for household items. Approximately four months after Amber left, Jack was good and getting used to his new life without her. He even came to me one day and said, "You know, Ma, I am getting so used to Amber being gone that she is not a part of my everyday thoughts anymore."

I was so proud of Jack because he had come a long way from the first day Amber left. Now, he had a new apartment and invited me to go furniture shopping with him. He had also picked out a 75-inch TV for his new pad. Jack was feeling much better, and I could see a smile on his face again! Hearing Jack say this and seeing him moving on from this toxic relationship was a joyful moment for me.

Jack had his apartment, his new furniture, and a TV scheduled for delivery that weekend. Because he had to work that weekend, the plan was for me to go to the apartment to be there for the delivery of all his new furniture. He was excited about his new place; we were talking about it and the upcoming holiday for we had been invited to a family dinner. Things were looking like they would be okay.

Chapter 18.

The Final Days of Jack's Life

Jack was doing well until one night, he and I were sitting and talking in the front room when he heard a text come through on his phone. When he looked at it, he didn't recognize the number. "I wonder who this is?" he said aloud as he opened the message that read:

"Heads up. Amber is going to the house tomorrow to move her stuff." It was from Teri. After reading the message, I noticed that Jack was suddenly quiet.

"What's wrong?" I asked.

I Choose You!!

He told me what the message said, which clearly bothered him. He asked me if I thought he should go to the house to speak with Amber to find out if that was what she really wanted. I advised Jack that it was my belief that this was just another one of Amber and her sisters' plots to get a rise out of him. Remember, she had been threatening for months to move her stuff from the home.

But now, because Jack did not budge or respond to her previous text messages, she figured it was time to take more drastic measures to get him to chase her again. She decided she would provoke Jack by actually giving an actual day of moving her stuff from the home.

{Side Bar: Amber had a key to the house, just like Jack did. Therefore, there was no reason for her to announce that she was moving her things from the house other than to f--k with Jack!}

Jack stayed overnight with me the day the message came through. By the morning, he seemed somewhat sad. I suspected this was mainly because he knew the day had finally come for Amber to move her things from the home. To make Jack feel somewhat better, I started talking about the upcoming events, including his new apartment that he already had keys to, his new furniture that was being delivered that week, and the family holiday dinner that we both planned to attend.

I knew Jack was concerned about his stuff that was still at the house. Knowing this, I told him that once Amber had moved her things from the house that day, he and I could go over the next day to make sure all his stuff was still there. This seemed to make Jack feel better, and he went off to work. The next morning, I made us pancakes and bacon, and then we headed over to the house. We talked along the way, and he seemed to be in a much better spirit.

When we turned the corner, we could see balloons floating from a garbage dumpster. As we got closer, we realized that this dumpster was in front of Jack's house. It looked like the dumpster had been intentionally placed in the front yard!

Jack and I got out of the car and saw that the balloons were ones that he had bought Amber. We approached the porch, walked up the stairs, and Jack opened the front door. As Jack opened the door, we were stopped because right there in front of the door was a shattered picture of Jack and Amber!

It looked like someone had *purposely* slammed and shattered the picture right in front of the door so that it would be the first thing he would see when he walked in. We both noticed the shattered picture and looked at each other like, "What the hell?" And, more importantly, "WHY?!"

After getting past the shattered photo, we went through the house to make sure none of his belongings were missing. Jack did notice that there were a few small things, such as a blender and a toaster, that belonged to him wasn't there, but he said they were no big deal and if she needed those small items *that* bad, she could *have* them.

He was mostly concerned about his appliances and barbecue grill that he had sold on the internet, and the person who bought them was coming to pick them up the next day.

Because Jack had to be at work shortly, we left the house without taking anything. Also, he was planning on moving his things the following day in preparation for his new apartment.

Shortly after returning to my house, Jack headed off to work, and the day went on as usual. Around an hour before it was time for Jack to get off work, he called me to say that he just received another text message from Teri stating, "Everything has been moved from the house, and for him to contact the property owner and let him know."

{Side Bar: Amber knew the property owner, just as Jack did. She would have contacted the owner or let her spokeswoman call him. *There was no reason to even say this to Jack outside of trying to F—k with him again!*

Anyway, I said to Jack, "What does she mean *everything* has been moved? She moved her stuff yesterday!" There was no reason for her to go back to the house. This was evidenced by the shattered picture in front of the door. No one who is moving is going to shatter a picture in front of the door if they *know* they're coming back to the house to get more stuff. She was just upset because the text message about her moving her stuff did not move Jack to the point of him running after her!

Nevertheless, once Jack saw the message on his phone, he could not wait to get off work to go see what else had been moved from the house—especially since Amber had previously gone to the house the day before to move *her* things. Jack was curious to know what Teri meant when she said *"everything"* had been moved from the house.

When Jack got off work, he headed straight to the house. Jack opened the door and entered the house; it was a horrific moment for both of us. Amber and whoever had helped her had taken *all* of Jack's stuff from the house, including his barbecue grill.

He called me on the phone so upset, saying she had taken all his things from the house; the house was clean with nothing left. I could tell that Jack was coming unhinged. He was running through the house screaming, "They took all my stuff!! They took all of my stuff!!"

I kept yelling at Jack through the phone to come to me. All I could do was yell, "Get out of there and come here! NOW!"

My mind was racing, and I felt so helpless on the other end of the phone. This conniving ass woman and her sister had pulled the coup de grâce on Jack, and I was trying to get him out of that house!

After screaming at Jack for about 10 minutes

to get out of there, he finally got into his car and headed my way. He kept saying, "Amber could not move those big items. She had other men in my house touching my stuff." This put a fire in Jack that I didn't know what to do with.

Once Jack got to my house and I opened the door, I could see he was at his wit's end. He came inside, and we were standing in the living room looking at each other. He was so gone that when I looked into his eyes, I could see there was something different about him. He had a look that made me realize that it was going to take more than just me to get Jack through this.

The horrifying reality was Jack did not have any male mentors in his life. His dad had died, and my brother, who I knew would be there for him, had passed away some years earlier. I was worried for my child, so I just kept talking and talking to him, trying to calm him down.

After 4-5 hours of talking with Jack, he

seemed to have relaxed. "Ma," he said softly, "You have to be at work in the morning. Go to bed."

"I know I have to be at work in the morning, but I want to make sure you're good before I lie down," I said to him with a yawn.

"Oh, Ma, I'm good," he reassured me. "I'm just going to take a shower and go to bed." He said he was tired from working all day.

"Okay, baby. I guess I will take a nap and see you in the morning."

I headed to my room and started to lie down. The house was quiet, and I started drifting off to sleep at the sound of Jack's shower running. A few moments later, I heard my bedroom door open, and it was Jack.

"Good night, Ma, I love you."

"I love you too, sweetheart," I said sleepily. "Don't worry, we will get this situation straightened out in the morning."

"Okay," he said as he turned around and

shut the door behind him. Little did I know, that was the LAST time I would see my beautiful Jack alive!

Chapter 19.

My Jack is Gone

I woke up a few hours later around 7 a.m. and started thinking about what I was going to wear to work that day. As I was thinking about that, my phone suddenly rang. I picked it up and saw it was Jack. When I saw it was him, I wondered why he was calling me when he was supposed to be in there sleeping. A strange feeling came over me as I answered.

Once I answered, I could hear Jack's voice on the other end saying to me, "I'm sorry, Ma, I fucked up!"

I Choose You!!

"NO! PLEASE NO!" I screamed, cutting him off mid-sentence. "What did you do?"

He told me what happened and that he loved me and then he hung up!

I frantically tried to call Jack back several times, but he did not answer. I started calling other family members to see if they had heard from Jack, but no one had heard from him.

I called and called and called, and then finally Jack answered. I asked him where he was, and he said he was just driving. He then started talking about how he wanted to go be with my mother, Aunt Ana, my brother, his dad, and his youngest brother.

I pleaded with Jack to please not say that because all of those family members he mentioned were deceased. Jack told me that he loved me and that he had to go, but he would call me back. I sobbed profusely on the phone, saying, "Please, Jack. Don't do anything. Please!" The phone went silent.

Now, I know you are probably wondering what Jack told me when he first called me that morning. Well, you see, after I fell asleep, Jack was alone with his thoughts of how Amber allowed other men to come into his home and take all of his things. This is the most important point he kept thinking about.

Once he convinced me to go the bed, he left, went to that house, and made his way through that same broken door that he had fixed some years earlier. Before entering the house, he noticed his barbecue grill and his appliances on the porch. He could also hear people talking and laughing inside the house, and he was livid. So, Jack entered the house, gunshots started ringing out, and those same people who just hours earlier were brave enough to enter Jack's house and remove his things started scattering. *Here* is where Amber met her demise.

As you can imagine, I was worrying, crying, and doing everything in my power to keep myself from having some form of mental breakdown at this point. I worried and waited for Jack to call me back.

The day had turned to night, and it had been hours since I had heard from my son. Then I saw a strange number on my phone. Figuring it was Jack, I immediately answered, but it was not Jack.

It was an unfamiliar voice on the other end identifying himself as a police officer. He asked for me by name, and when I answered that it was me speaking, he asked if he could come to my house to speak with me in person. At the time I was not at home, but I said yes and headed home.

About 30 minutes later, he along with another police officer came to my house and told me my Jack was GONE! My beloved beauty had taken his life!

CONCLUSION

As you can imagine, losing my Jack was devastating to no end. Knowing *how* and *why* he died made writing this book a challenge for me. When I initially thought of telling Jack's story to help other men avoid getting themselves into similar toxic situations, I was reluctant to do so because I knew that meant I would have to re-experience the details of what happened to my Jack and how I no longer have him here with me!

Although I had to stop several times to wipe my tears and nurse my broken heart over and over again, I continued on because my mission was and still is not to let Jack's life be gone in vain. My Jack was an educated, loving, honest, and caring man who got caught in a trap by a deceiving, disrespectful, conniving, unappreciative, toxic woman and her family.

He not only took on the relationship with Amber, but he took on the responsibility of a child whose father was nowhere to be found! And how does this woman thank Jack and show her appreciation for him? She doesn't! What she did was reveal how disrespectful, cunning, controlling, and devious she truly was. She always had to have one up on Jack.

When Jack didn't respond in the way she wanted him to after she ran off, she would take her detrimental antics to new levels. This is proven after she left the last time for the family house, and Jack made a decision not to beg her to come back and instead let her come home on her own. As you read in Jack's story, he did everything in his power to get Amber to come home. However, after rejection and embarrassment after rejection and embarrassment, Jack felt defeated and shut down from the whole situation.

After realizing Jack was not over there at that house begging her to come home and that it was possible he had left her undeserving toxic ass alone for real, the first text message came, threatening to move her things from the house. Then she figured, "Oh, that didn't get your attention? How about I take it up a notch."

The next text message came, threatening to have the cable and lights shut off. When she could not get Jack to come running after her with these threats, she and the trifling toxic relationship advisor Teri figure, "Oh, those two threats didn't work? How about this."

The next message came with an actual day of Amber moving her things from the house. Since Jack was *still* not responding, she figured, "Oh, okay then. I will *show* you better than I can *tell* you." So, she followed through with that threat and actually moved her stuff from the house. Oh, but before she left, what did she do to try to inflict more pain on Jack? She shattered the picture of her and him at the front door's entrance!

After all the threats Amber made and even followed through on to Jack to get a reaction out of him, Jack still didn't respond. Getting no response from Jack, she then decided to commit the ultimate diabolical act in an effort to get Jack to come after her, which was gather up some people, go to Jack's house, and clean out all of *his* stuff.

Afterward, what did she do? Oh, she made sure Jack *knew* his stuff was removed by having Teri send Jack the last and final message about everything being gone and for him to contact the landlord.

At this point, Amber got *exactly* what she was desperately seeking from Jack, which was for him to come to that house in pursuit of her; however, unfortunately for her and my Jack, the chase she was aiming for was not in the way she was *expecting*!

With all the things Amber and her family had done to Jack, removing his belongings from his house was the breaking point. That night, when Jack went to his house and saw that Amber and whoever else she had in his house had removed all of his belongings, this caused him to spiral into a dark space.

The result of her actions was truly unthinkable for both of them! The most disturbing part of this devastating situation is that when Jack was gone, I road past that family house and saw firsthand that all of Jack's things were right there on the porch. This evil woman didn't even have room in that house to put Jack's stuff. She just took them out of SPITE!

MEN, here is a note to self: if these toxic women are not wise enough to know when to stop taunting and playing with a man's mind, emasculate, or control him, then it is *your* responsibility to be intelligent enough and in tune with yourself to detect this behavior in these women early. You must be aware when you are dealing with a woman who could be detrimental to your well-being.

Also men, as a woman and a mother, I can tell you that some of us were raised up in a normal, loving environment. However, there are *some* who were snatched up in the streets. The only things most of them know about being in a relationship with a man are dogging (emasculating) him, getting his money, and doing whatever they can to control him!

Knowing this, you have to be on the lookout for certain types of behavior being displayed early in the wooing stage of a relationship, so I have outlined some RED FLAGS from Jack's story for you to be aware of.

Red Flags!

1. The first RED FLAG is to trust your gut feelings, aka your male intuition. If your spirit is telling you something is not right with the person when you first meet them, don't do it! I'm sure Jack had these feeling, but oh, that Jezebel spirit was at its best in convincing Jack to take her back and that things would be different!

2. The second RED FLAG stood out early in Jack's story with the whole "I Choose You" statement from Amber. She deceived Jack into believing she was something special by telling him she had a waiting list of men to

choose from. Jack, being in his 20s, bought into deceitfulness when in reality, she knew Jack was a guy who was not from the streets. She knew he liked her and that she could use this lie to give herself more leverage from the start of her BS.

3. The third RED FLAG is if you go to meet a woman at her house, and the closer you get to her home, the more run down and destitute the area becomes. This is an opportunity for you to keep driving right on by and be a no-call no-show. If the area she lives in is in the shape, it's highly likely that her behavior and mindset are also in this form! Keep driving!

4. The fourth RED FLAG happened after Jack went to meet Amber and her family in person at her house. He was treated poorly by her in front of her family. If a woman shows you blatant disrespect when you first meet, cut

your losses early and do NOT stick around for another dose of that ish. As you read from Jack's story, after the first disrespectful encounter, Jack experienced and went on his way. Amber *conned* her way back into his life, and it got even worse with the whole birthday party rachetness. Don't allow this to be you!

5. The fifth RED FLAG was when she pressured Jack into moving into an apartment with her and her child to get away from her family while not having a job! No job, no check, which means all the financial responsibility will fall on you!

6. The sixth RED FLAG was when Amber's jealousy reared its head with Jack's job offer. Men, women can be jealous of you, and you will not even know it! Even for the simplest things you would not even imagine, for example, Amber was jealous when Jack

would get dressed up, even if it was just casual wear like jeans and a nice sweater. She would find something wrong with him: he had a piece of lint on him, or his hair wasn't right. She would even make comments like, "Where did you get that from?" while laughing, as to imply that he looked silly or stupid in some way. When you experience a woman downplaying your wins, your looks, or always finding something wrong with you, it's a possibility that this woman is low-key jealous of you!

7. The seventh RED FLAG is if you've noticed her behavior towards you has changed, and she turns little nothings into massive somethings. The next thing you know, she's out the door! The out-the-door part is what she was aiming for in the first place. It's time to keep a heightened eye on this situation and possibly start your exit plan!

8. The eighth Red Flag is when the woman you're dating is allowing her family or girlfriends aka troublemakers, too much access to the relationship. It's also a major flag if she allows them to make it seem like she's incapable of making her own decisions. For example, Amber allowed Teri to inject herself straight into her and Jack's relationship. She couldn't see that this woman had left her husband, came home to find that she had found her a good man, became jealous, and set out to destroy her relationship with Jack. Amber was already toxic enough on her own; she for damn sure didn't need any outside influences. If you find the person you are with has outside influences that are detrimental to the relationship and she can't seem to get this addressed accordingly, it's time to start your EXIT plan!!

9. Another RED FLAG is intentionally trying to make you jealous of how she

chooses to dress and go out in public. This is what Amber would do, especially when she would go out without Jack. I'm not sure *why* she wanted to test Jack in this way. It may be because she knew how much he cared for her and was trying to get a jealous reaction from him. He showed her how much he cared for her, so this behavior was unnecessary! Men, how a woman dresses in public when she's in a relationship is important for two reasons. 1) It shows the public that she respects herself and her man to not come out the house looking slutty, and 2) It alleviates you as the man from having to get into an altercation with other men who might be looking/catcalling at the slutty dressed women causing you to feel upset or angry possibly! If she wants to go out dressed this way, you have a right not to put yourself in danger and not go!

10. The most important RED FLAG of all

is if you choose to or find yourself incidentally falling in love with a woman, make sure the woman is mature and responsible enough for you to give her your heart. Do you trust her with such a pivotal part of you? Do you trust that she will be responsible enough to do the right thing with it? If you are not sure about these questions, you might want to hold on until you can answer "Yes!"

Final Thoughts

It has taken me some time to deal with Jack's death, but once I got to a place of figuring out how to cope with the loss and pain of him being gone, I felt it was my responsibility to share Jack's story with other men. I know Jack is not the only man who has encountered this type of negative spirit whose only mission was to destroy him, which is what she did in the absolute end!

In sharing Jack's story, I am most hopeful that it will bring light to these types of relationships and save the lives of other men and women. The lives of two people who should have NEVER met were snuffed out by the conniving, selfishness, and naivety of a woman who allowed her ignorance to not only steer her to her death but my Jack to his death as well.

Jack's situation with this woman caused him to lose his life in a way I have seen and heard so many times before. He should still be here as should so many other men who naively fell victim to this pit hole of not knowing the signs that a "Man Trap" was being set for them! I have provided several Red Flags to be on the lookout for when searching in these social media streets for the right woman. I never want another mother to have to bury her beloved son because of an evil-spirited woman he should have NEVER met!

Disclaimer: I am not a licensed therapist or counselor, but I am a Life Change Agent. If you are in a toxic relationship and want out, I will do my best to help you and or your loved one get their life back and avoid more heartache and pain, and more importantly avoid the unthinkable death.

If you or someone you love is in a toxic relationship or just need some relationship advice, you can reach out to me at jacksjourneyspeaks@gmail.com. I will be more than happy to help you get your life back!

Also, if you or anyone you know is facing troubles and are thinking of harming yourself or anyone else, **please contact the suicide hotline at 988.**

Sam Troy

I Choose You!!

Sam Troy

www.ingramcontent.com/pod-product-compliance
Lightning Source LLC
LaVergne TN
LVHW041256080426
835510LV00009B/752